MARA'S SHADE

NEW WORLD TRANSLATION SERIES, NUMBER 1

New World Translation Series
Editors, Christopher Merrill and David St. John

Cover image: iStockphoto.com
Author photo: Dimitris Tsoublekas

Design, layout: Tania Baban, Jim Natal, Conflux Press

ISBN 13: 978-1-893670-72-3
ISBN 10: 1-893670-72-4

Library of Congress Control Number: 2010943432

A Tebot Bach book

Tebot Bach, Welsh for little teapot, is A Nonprofit Public Benefit Corporation which sponsors workshops, forums, lectures, and publications. Tebot Bach books are distributed by Small Press Distribution, Armadillo and Ingram.

THE TEBOT BACH MISSION

Tebot Bach is dedicated to strengthening community, promoting literacy, and broadening the audience for poetry by demonstrating through readings, workshops, and publications, the power of poetry to transform human experience.

This book is made possible by a grant from The San Diego Foundation Steven R. and Lera B. Smith Fund at the recommendation of Lera Smith.

www.tebotbach.org

MARA'S SHADE

SELECTED POEMS
1971-1995

ANASTASSIS VISTONITIS

Translated from the Greek by
David Connolly

With an Introduction by
Christopher Merrill

TEBOT BACH • HUNTINGTON BEACH • CALIFORNIA

TABLE OF CONTENTS

INTRODUCTION
By Christopher Merrill

Anastassis Vistonitis occupies a unique position in Greek letters: equally acclaimed as a poet and a journalist, he switches from one medium to the other with seeming ease, now composing poems and literary essays, now turning out book reviews and articles, often on the same day. Both streams feed the sea of his imagination—he calls his prose a continuation of poetry by other means—and his Greek readers are fortunate to have his work available to them in so many forms. He has published eleven collections of poetry, three volumes of essays, four travelogues, a book of stories, and a translation of the Chinese poet Li Ho; he edits and writes for the book section of *To Vima*, the leading newspaper; he even assembled the candidature file for the Athens Olympics, articulating the argument that convinced the International Olympic Committee to return the Games to their original site. Indeed his work is a testament to the ancient Greek idea of the intimate connection between the body and the soul. What good luck to have a selection of his poems in English, in the splendid translation of David Connolly.

Vistonitis cuts a large figure, both in his presence and on the page. He was born in 1952 in Komotini, near the Turkish border, and when an injury cut short a promising soccer career he threw himself into poetry, coming of age during the military dictatorship (1967-1974). His early work is marked by the artistic, intellectual, and political ferment of the time, and it is no accident that in his subsequent writings he exhibits a deep understanding of the relationship between literature and politics (he studied political science and economics in Athens); also a grasp of the world beyond Greece. He traveled extensively in Europe, Africa, and Asia, lived in New York and Chicago, where he perfected his English, and schooled himself in several literary traditions, ever mindful of the ethical dimension of his craft. His work is dense with allusion and insight, as befits one of the best-read writers of the age, and in these poems he displays not only a range of theme but also formal possibilities, from variations on Byzantine prosody to prose poems to lyrical meditations. Readers will instantly recognize the voice of a major poet.

"From the Side of the Sea," for example, opens with a series of apocalyptic versets:

It was night when we descended the narrow path to the sea
No wind was blowing just as yesterday. Lights were mirrored

in a black glass. In it we saw our faces' negatives.

Far off appeared the flickers of a huge fire.

This is where we'll stay till morning, I said, and the others didn't speak. Another land began where the fire was fading and no one knew it. No one knew if what was burning was the great palace, as the day's rumors had it, or gleams of a glory burning in time. Someone suggested we go to find the ash remaining before the wind scattered it.

Always there's a sea intervening, said one of the others, with his voice covering his face. We, too, could start a fire and burn the sea. Glass doesn't burn and what you see is not the sea.

The speaker, who claims to have been born with a glass eye, goes on to raise questions—"Who is the night, what is the night, left right, O left right"—and pose hypothetical solutions: "If I were to jump, I'd find myself at the other edge of the sky, if I turned around. If…" He means to discover his bearings in a place that has not been mapped before and a time that demands a more accurate form of measurement than conventional literary practice offers. The situation is dire, and yet the very surge of these lines suggests that an imaginative response is possible—which, if nothing else, may make our walk in the sun more bearable. The poem thus concludes with an image— "The ruins of the fire in the palace began to set"—that in its seeming finality promises nevertheless that another sun will rise, another occasion to light the darkness.

This is what distinguishes Vistonitis: his determination to grasp the meaning of the fact, as he writes in a poem titled "1968," that he is but "a fragment of all that [he has] encountered." Whether exploring China, traveling on a train from Lisbon to St. Petersburg in the company of a hundred poets and writers, or reflecting on the achievement of literary figures from around the globe, he brings to bear an exacting and exuberant intelligence. "Nightmarish imagination," he proclaims in the last line of this book: "you are not yourself, you are not, you are not." Indeed it is other, it is the language itself, and in these poems it speaks for all of us, lighting the way.

from:
EMIGRATING
1971-1972

LETTER

Or on the reduction of events

I

The river a steel surface
covered with a silver layer of ice.
The city—a dark grapple in the void.
Above the useless stars,
above the moon
flat lights like knives slashed her body.

We sat on the stone ledge—motionless
statues—in a musical sorrow.

We stood again in the same place for what we loved:
for the large city that opened up the marvel before us,
for the narrow streets that became a tight mesh
—splintered glass in our faces.

II

Now as I write to you the water is running out, the light
       is running out.
A bronze bird scars me with its claws
and the state's cold hand crushes me.
I am not the wooden body on the table
for I recall the steel river at our feet,
the face of the city with the rotted buildings
that sowed memory's sickness within us.
Friend
the voices approaching come from another world,
far beyond the harsh wall of darkness,
far beyond the faces that were once beside us
yet faded now by time and sadness.

III

Shipwrecked in the port at dawn
with the rotting sailboats and the ships' dogs
glaring fiercely at sea and sky,
between the crushed timbers and the pebbles
masts sticking up like ancient spears
and a fragment of gunwale from the Persian boat
with the mark of Cynosoura's teeth.

IN WAIT

Space diminishes in a room.
Shipwrecks—degenerate dreams.

Some will climb the ladder.
Carnivorous smiles.

Outside it will be raining—a flat rain.

The room will be a narrow garment
and the heart a newspaper thrown on the floor.

The woman on the wall will fray.
Her rotting eyes will gaze at you.

As on the horizon
the town will grow distant.

Without portents, without signs.

SUNDAY

Sunday, a day for children.

The same room.
Memory's journey.

The same insect contre lumière.

Sunday, a day for children,
bathed in the blood of Saturday.

ENFIN

Just the two of us remained and the light.

If those are two pale plants
in the window tormented
by the night and the chains,
I feel their lamentation merged
like an amalgam of darkness and grief.

For you asked of me so much
an entire life
so that now the time cries out
so that now we clutch hands
in a past of murdered images
and children forgotten
in the earth's dark womb
and the despondency of age.

ARS POETICA

A poem is not like the leaves
swept by the wind in the streets.
It is not the still sea,
the moored boat.
It is not the blue sky
and a clear atmosphere.

A poem is a spike
in the heart of the world.
A gleaming knife
plunged straight in the towns.
A poem is anguish,
a piece of shining metal,
ice, a dark wound.
A poem is hard,
a polyhedral diamond.
Solid—sculpted marble.
Rushing—an Asian river.

A poem is not a voice,
the passing of a bird.
It is a gunshot
into the horizon and history.
A poem is not a flower that withers.
It is embalmed pain.

From:

SCOUTS

1972-1974

ILLUSION

Fantasy of the suicide of Sergey Yesenin, Leningrad 1925.

I
It is not just fever's veins—
a gunpowder sun blasts me.

On other nights the Trans-Siberian passed
outside the window crossing
wooden Russia.

The veins enslaved rivers—
leave towards the Volga.
In the horizon's red flash
I see—drunken phantoms
board the ship
crossing the murderous waters.

II
The striking of the blade in the flesh,
this is what you should fear, crazy drunk,
not your mind's rotten peel.
....
Dusk is a steppe
of vodka and a tavern's sounds.
Dusk opens the door for me—
Abraham's rotten teeth.

III
When young I watched in winter's necropolis
the trees' skeletons speaking
fashioning notes from the wind's voice,
then wolves from the Baltic,
walking rags from the wounds of the Caucasus—
cracked winter's crust.
Their fevered hands
beside my mother's embrace,
in a land bereft of sun.

I pass through the dark gate.
As the rope tightens
two red cannons
bombard my eyes.

THE ROBBERS

The first in the wood

The wood is a green flag
that unveils night's fires
along the shaded paths, as the song
leaps from the inferno of their eyes.
Freedom—a volcano spouting
unrestrained cries and gunshots.

The nightingales' terror fills the night
with sounds from the chestnuts. Laughter
falls silent in the woodlands.
In the town the gendarmes huddle
with the holed-up mice.
My knife the harp of death.
I pin the light on the branches at midday.

From out of their mouths fly
hungry hawks.
The unsaddled horses bolt toward the peaks,
from out of the sky fall coins
and bloated kings.

In my heart the night plants
a plane tree of granite.

The second in jail

My horse flies through the gorges
chasing the morning bells.
Pale women beneath the moon
slip on the riverbank.
My heart beats in my horse's hooves.
In the town the tightfisted
nail shut their windows.
Waiting for me at dawn is a wall
or a noose in the square.

Gendarmes roam the streets
with their buttons and pistols.

Night leads me to the lands of the South.
At dawn I set fire to my house
and depart for the other world.

The third on the scaffold

At one end of the rope the light,
at the other a deep red memory.
The children toss my cask
—black ship—into the river.
Ah, those rivers full of wine
and northern songs.
And then the calm and awesome sea.
I emerge from a rusted world.

CRIME ON THE RIVER

It's red and red doesn't show the blood so much.
DOSTOYEVSKY

Willows enmeshed in the river's mud,
Tadpoles' bodies, dirt and black death.
The moon passes through the branches
lighting the birds' sleep.
Willows—a line of fear and expectation
and above a galaxy pouring forth lime.
The city an army of candles and light breeze.
Knives of ice in the water's mirror
and in the mind the sound of a heavy cart.
Darkness, path to the clouds—
the water growing stale in the rivers.

The night a heavy pebble.
Someone is traveling on the northbound trains.
He is waiting and smoking.
At night the clouds set up roadblocks
and stop the birds' flights.
Round the lights in the parks mad insects
jostle in the white glare.

The city—phantom of a nocturnal downpour,
a child's broken toy.
Threads of the willow trees, gaps
so the moon may pass, white wax,
leaving the clouds and gripping the trees.
On the thick trunk bark like an old man's skin.
A heavy axe buried in it. The wood
a dead wolf's sealed mouth.

THE MORROW

Forged light in a fearful night.
A burning tiger the fierceness
slashes my skin.
In pursuit the other birds
smell wall and darkness.
Their opium-filled eyes wildlings in the plain.

Between the city and my face
the window's glass river
riddled with machines that perform
the actions of madmen.

The night has duration in time—
a black flame from iron candles
whose wick is an ambush.
………..

Day has broken.
The streets open wide.
The stone creaks from the light.
The sea's armor.

I vanish into day's raw whiteness.

BECALMED

A sober day at the window.
I am immobilized in a vessel
stuck fast to the quay.

The railings on the horizon
are ravaged by the silent rains.
The light stirs the objects
and my grey eyes.
A waste of worthless color
midday—no one is hounding me.

from:

ALONE
(Poems to Edgar Allen Poe)
1975

ALONE

*...I could not bring
my passions from a common spring*
E.A. POE

I
The music a huge, red
moon traveling in the hills.

I cannot live in the black hole,
a mad shadow at night
snatches the trees and roofs—
the unknown passing death

The night returns,
the ancient pendulum,
blind and certain fear.

In the hole of my self candescent
time burns my innards.

II
The rain is a frozen drum
and my soul a morning shiver.
Through the lethargy the light rises
like a summer moon.

On my cold eyelids the day
a blue rose opens
its sky.

III
Ghosts of lines, silver-plated sorrow,
tears of love's passions,
compression of the world into a space without light,
music and pain of things,
iridescences and shadows of youth.

Edgar Allan Poe
in a Baltimore tavern
in his inebriation's tempest
staggers and caresses the cosmos.

ANNABEL LEE

Your eyes.
A winter descends
with frosts and downpours.
Lonely graveyards strip themselves
of dust and strangers' footsteps.
Rain—blood of stars and flowers,
blood of the body.

Your eyes hollowed walls—
a foreign army passes.
The shiver of the breeze over the sea.

The wrinkles faded in the future.
Night writhes in the empty coffin
going deeper even than the light,
sky buried in the earth,
the humming of time within
the shore's empty skull,
reflection by the seaweed
that becomes a candle to light
the subterranean currents and darkness.

Your eyes.
Full of death and epidemic.

From:
ASHES
1975-1977

SHOOTING RANGE

The midday is shattered.
Unburied dead light.
The sea encircles the horizon.

Shadows facing the sun
and day—the predatory river.

You hear the talk. Somewhere else
the crowd thickens, steeled
within the opened city
and the sun static and yellow—
a shining chair
in the center of the sky.

NON EST

Deserted streets, yellow horizon,
empty chairs and his footsteps.
A hidden fever eats at the city.
Diffuse light, faded blood.
He twists his fingers in his pocket,
feels his mind evaporating,
pigheaded, ready to ignite,
a wounded day, he whispers slowly,
footsteps, again footsteps, far from the street,
footsteps far from the footsteps.

Hell is a city much like London…

The sun—a stuffed hawk.
The sea—a wall of water.
The paralyzing light trembles in the distance,
cars cross the place,
shadows, motionless streets, buildings.

Loss of rhythm,
a word that closes like an oyster
and then the slaughterhouse-memory
red, hemophoric, blackens
in his dark gaze that leaves
for other seas beyond.

He seeks again the stimulus
as the light strips him,
as the day tightens its noose around his neck.

OPEN THE GATES

Window of glass and plaster.
In the mist danced
phantoms and angels.
Planning death
he recalled the memory.
The insidious step,
the sudden creaking,
starting to live again
cowardly friends and unseen enemies.

Sick now in a distant hospital
he declares a false identity.
With a deadly gaze he watches the evening
swallowing him.

TEN PAST ONE

Flat roofs, suspended balconies,
slow blinking of lights behind curtains.
Inside my head a sail is flapping
and the night dyes it black.
A moon-struck cloud descends.
Sleep wraps me in its white asphalt.

THE WOODCUTTER'S VIGIL

The door open to the large forest.
The moon square in the chimney
full of shadows and shaking windows.
Not a whisper. Only the darkness creeping
deep into my skull fills me with colors.
Silver in the scanty light the walls' wood
keeps yesterday's wind moist.

Tomorrow I'll wake with a hostile dawn in my eyes.
The trees will return to a land of forgetting.
A sun all of snow will transport me.

FOUR POINTS

POINT I
When a red cloud sets
and the evening is a dark,
naked body of a shadow in terror,
when it smells of approaching rain,
the death rattle of a leaf
can be heard amid the glass trees.

Multistoried and dark the sun
—memory's catacomb—
enters the earth.

POINT II
I recall your oaken eyes.
A mist was falling,
colors and fever
and the rivers' wide cloth
that crosses time
unloosed in myriads of droplets
airy amid the greenery.

From your oaken eyes the light
leaps shaking
its steely straightness.

POINT III
The well in the yard
is a mournful sun
accompanying my funeral.

That bare tree shows me
the immortality of bones.

If I remove my eyes
I'll see a negative landscape.

POINT IV
Your eyes have the gleam of swords,
your arms are two shoots of black heather,

the valley of your legs is a birds' graveyard
and your blood a sea of red seaweed.

I watch your moonstruck hair twirling
in a cold and foggy night.
On your words dances a mad Mara
and like a pomegranate time opens and scatters.

THE MOON IN THE GLASS

I
This
unsteady table
polarizes the wilderness, recalls dead friends.
With a lamp it freezes the darkness.

Yet the light is not like that.

I saw it as a boy in the plains
emerging from the colors,
round moon, map of springs,
above the maize and wheat.

II
Now
the midnight chill
is a stone inscription above the houses,
and the sea a place of invisible breathing.
Impasses, painful decisions,
the wasted blood of loved ones,
this table fills with wooden teeth,
burnt masks, shadows that flame
and in the middle a glass of water
with the moon sunk at the bottom.

EVENING: COLD AND CLOUDY

With fear's crimson fragment stuck in our heads
and our eyes split wide,
the afternoon's tin skies resound,
the skies we loved
in the most dangerous of our dreams.

Presence is wasted in useless discourse.
Behind the iciness of ideas,
to a rhythm of harsh repulsion, ascends
what separates me from others.

What cuts and throws my self into the street,
the line, my butchered smile,
sunk in a despondent environment—
that's how I met you at night,
with my mind thundering inside its shell,
my peeled sense,
the linear phantom of the past
with a rasping cough rending the air.

Leaning to right and left
in blue rain
and a collapsing sky.

DELIRIUM TREMENS

I
Darkness, cement and fire.
The ashen fog-gauze on the streets.
The enormous tragedy of the dream
transforms the town into its reflection.
The winter passed with silicon rains,
marks in the grooves, rickety doors,
supports, feelings, fundamental laws,
the afternoon, glass coated in X color,
apart from you, your long-lasting fever,
in a fit of elation and intimations
the barren memory   shipwrecks.

II
Stones radiate, the dust light,
in the leafage the glittering shatters
cracking the dark prisms.
Rivers, magnetic waves,
crime scene without weapons,
the stains, the holes, the sack
supporting your head…
The wood with the rusty nails…
The whitewash's white pits…
Shadows bisected ad infinitum…
The icons' cardinal value,
the sidewalk cracked under the steps.
Swallowing blazing darkness
you feed the night, your gnawed face,
you feed the other who gnaws you.

III
The barren memory   shipwrecks.
Climbing up to myself
in a bland range, with preceding
your plant cell, dead in yesterday,
a microbe enlarged and monstrous.
Ants crawl in your blood.
Your eye targets the wall,
your arm targets your eye,

a plaything of living vertebrae,
disorderly you roll into feverish nothing,
with the horizon cutting you in two,
till next year,
till the shadows.

IV
In pieces beneath the present
dawns tomorrow.
You wear a descendent, his marks
are imprinted in your images:
Patches of filth.
Iron.
Light.

From:

GROUND

1977-1979

DREAM

All my life I never had anything.
Yet now they've taken everything from me.

Here—thousands of others. I too become another
searching to find another.
A scattered pile of what once constituted me.

My face uncertain, the system
a series of indistinct lines.

He doesn't notice the disfigurement.
He doesn't know. Even one single grimace
may shatter the world. For last night
I awoke and the darkness around
was a lyrical landscape, a raging spring,
and I saw enormous blooms chewing the walls.
The white wind took me up to its sky.

GAZE

The voiceless morning. Stationery cars. From here to there without there being any there. Gloomy and scared all of us with an imperceptible trembling just at the edge.

You will escape the trauma, go beyond the sensation, to the so-called depth.

Thick and fluid, the light creeps over our faces.

I turned and gazed into the mist. The grass was silver, leaden and blue, passed through faint yellow strips and the old mountain inaccessible in its ashes. Everything would have been dream-like, if not for the weapons.

METAPHOR

After years I see the stars again.
Moonless night, mother of monsters,
a sky full of eddies,
electric rivers, valleys,
shadows of fever and trenches
in the back of the skull.
White images come—
the pale color of illusions.

Summer full of mould and cigarettes
and for fifty years now only trash.

Your voice, your breath, fine
line of a spider and your soul
an insect hanging in the void.

Within me trembles an old fantasy.

REVERSAL

After the rain, the wind-glass strips the world. Crossing an empty space, lonely discarded trees—goodbye to all old things. Yesterday, others came to me in my sleep babbling about forests and towns abandoned in the snow. Yet their eyes were red and their hair white and sleep a harmful tree full of insects. Termites in the earth opened that hole through which the fruit will be spoiled, the enemies will be annihilated, the struggle with the rock-wheat will take place.

The girl with the matches a woman in revolt, red from the flame of her passion. Now there's a meaning. She's called Rosa.

Hidden in my eye is a grim image, a ravaged landscape with crumbling materials, a mind made ash that thinks by itself, refusing to move limbs not belonging to it.

I step on a ladder,
close my eyes,
dream of a wild river.

WIND

After so much rain the sky opens, the stars come out.
Clouds of grey snow and in their midst the moon.
Your eyes moist like spring's weeping.
Spring and yet cold and an aged wind
and your thought chafing at the present.

Almost nothing. Or rather
a slight crack, a wrinkle
on the image's surface. It came and went. Just that.

We got to know each other well this winter.
In your face is reflected my own shadow,
better that you don't speak, better that you listen with your innards.
Like a child.
Leave the others there in the ditch—and even lower.

Mildly, very mildly, like color fading,
like the hand making a slow movement in space,
like snow melting in the hand,
like just before you fall asleep.

If I halt I'll hear the blood's beat
and returning the sound of the earth
moved by the plants' radical grasp,
and the fate-root descends,
the alchemy that turns darkness into light,
this, the scattering,
        the blossoming.
I begin falling into myself,
in a foreign landscape, in a charred forest.
My thought is the last living insect,
and therefore irrational and enflamed.

Now I should emerge from the night
with the step of a burglar—
I am consumed by a passionate nature,
an unbridgeable sky, a rusted horizon
and with the others coming from afar
offering earth and water, ancient credentials,
and to whom? To those depraved of old.

WATER AND OIL

If time passes all will be forgotten,
the night, the bitter water, the gallows on the horizon,
a man who apparently was dead awoke
in the wrong universe—so much mud? you ask.
Because the ground is sticky underfoot,
the past an elastic gravity, forests and convoys,
low sea, opaque pearl, without descendents,
like a bad dog, dragging a life, a desolate rind.

Night, marine mother, squeeze me in your ash,
in the tree set the owl, the unripe leaf, my friends,
far from the blind realm of the living, that I may see with my hands,
hear with my skin, bite ice and wood
averting my gaze from this flattened landscape.

The darkness quivers in the brain,
the intimate, the apoplectic, the prehistoric moth,
and the water's erosive trickle on the floor
furrows the chrono-photographic darkness.
A drop of water and oil, winter and mould,
a little girl barely outlined in a mirror,
water and oil, mirror, cloth, window,
a framework of sky, stained years.
Don't regard my aging eye, my hand
eroded by the wind, water and oil.

If time passes all will be forgotten.
And what you heard one afternoon, a small house,
a creaking chair, clothes facing the door,
walls of flayed sky, a dead bird on the ceiling,
a stuffed hawk gazing at the night through the crack,
and the darkness swelling, and your tedium inaccessible,
a different winter stirs in your icy laughter,
a bewildered landscape, gazing cyclically at nothing,
a Sunday empty and absurd, chest buried
and your stupefied foot scratching the wall
just as the circle closes, as the passes narrow,
as long ago, there where a dry leaf is tossed,
a broken branch full of mist and water,

water and oil again tonight, be gone from here, there's
a road further down, a moon.

Darkness' crosswise movements in the night, your bloated body,
biting the old wound that feeds you,
you, an internally-burning, dark heir.

RIFLE-RANGE

A large blemish below the eye.
I see the world, the black square of the living,
time's ground plans, multiplicity, brightness and cloud.

I am gripped by a thought, a mild catastrophe, the night you disappeared,
you entered the period of age,
following an indistinct cycle,
suspicion and strife-pain, facts, privileges.

This, your own darkness, turns muddy.
Images stick to the face.
And where I encountered you the first time, in a prime moment,
consumption and glory of my youth,
room, and house and streets with trees.

A plundered melody,
a mind full of rain.

Walking again now in the waters
I'll torment my soul,
the thorny grass of childhood,
that fine thread cutting my throat,
one who's hoarse dying inside me,
tomorrow when the wall shines and silently
the phantom, the dark laughter of those absent, will fade.

GROUND, 1

About our blurred eyes
fly images of bad dogs,
ashes from yesterday's fire.
Deeper than the skin an emptiness,
phantoms of knowledge,
the dead chromosome
and the rock-time indivertible
rooted there—you here.

Tomorrow you'll set out,
planted in your skin the future
crawls and bites your flesh,
as you will gape in the opening,
tomorrow was a river
and now is only darkness.
Only darkness and sleepwalkers' steps,
sawn iron that tumbles
and afterwards nothing. And afterwards then.
For the time began to melt.
For the landscape began not to have
and a great death rattle took away your ears,
took away your hours, the fantasy of the future,
your tattered dress flapping,
the cascade piercing your thought
on such a night, a staked-out field
and over your head the sky—
a muddied cover.

GROUND, 2

It seemed I heard spring's radiant voice
on finding in the humidity formed images,
reflections and pangs, the birth beyond me, the rounded
fruit.

The ruins are ancient and yellowed.
You couldn't recall if ever you'd passed by here.
Everything is lit but nothing shines bright.
And the light stains your inner rift,
spring, rage of infants.

Passing into years back I again saw the river.
Not as the pass shrinks, the wind,
a barrage of dizziness.
So, the same again I reflect.
Once you knew me differently, I had a name,
my personal aversion.
Child, cradle of imagination—not in stone,
the cross, nailed surfaces,
your glinting iron eye,
the light hewing the landscape—around you fragments.

Around you fragments.
You made the decision not to return,
since next to you now passes delusion,
passes a lifeless body, a drained memory.

A bird of ash sown on the horizon.

SELF-ENSLAVED

After some years you'll have nothing to remember—
the paradisiacal image scatters in the wind,
the times and the darkness crush you.
You are obliged to vanish into the crowd—
a worm-eaten pawn.
Your phantom an extension of Hades
surrounded by murderers.

It's in this blood that you will fall and vanish
playing with the blood for years and years.
Your face a grimace of disgust,
an exotic venom
burdens the future within you,
a nocturnal wound full of fear and water
and with the wild hair of dead angels.

For murder escalates time,
the hideous darkness in the executioner's hands,
they bury the deceased as if he were a thing,
in his eyes flow cities and forests,
a river of dark constellations
your eye will open and break
and the descendent with the trash's rust
will emerge from the pile and will resemble you.

From:
JOURNALS
1971-1982

NOW YOU'RE ALONE...

In the first difficult night
without transparencies, digging the impossible,
without even an inkling of presence,
touching the earth,
those who came yesterday
may gaze at you tomorrow too
from the same wilderness.

No one knows you.
Amid the cold ash,
the weightless smoke,
swimming in a neutral ink
you seek a pretext,
a mark of recognition—
and the city is reflected in the window.

Now you're alone despite all the stars.
Beneath the lamp's curved light
burnt darkness falls before your eyes.
No one sees it. No one knows why
black hoarfrost falls from the sky
and you, why did you name
that useless material world.

A EGNATIA 1958

The street with its trash is visible again.
Litter and leaves mixed in the mud,
tin cans gaping open
and the afternoon red and yellow
melting in the atmosphere.
Pyrotechnic time.

The houses exude the smell of sulfur
mingled with damp earth and trash.

Down here the soothsayer sleeps,
over there the emaciated queen;
and just between the usurper,
the domestic dog guardian of the dead
with its wet ears pricked up—
harking to the darkness.

Dislocated town;
uninhabited years.
Carts still roll down.
Time creaks in their wheels,
summer passes like something sour.
cracked wall, whitewash, dust, disemboweled barrels.

To live with a gnawed brain, here—
the evening falling the darkness predatory,
your body surrendered.
with square eye you play the window and the sky
in an animal absolute,
expanses of the unconscious.

Street, illness and bugbear,
the body's burden,
excavated past,
irreparably redeemed,
dry wound that's rubbed and scatters.

Memory, monument, months that passed
leaving behind invasion's tatters,
remains of a chair,

a mangled table
and light fragments from the sky,
memory's mute and absolute computation.

Many. So many.
And a totally cerebral echo,
a thought that happens again,
unbearable and empty,
exhaustingly, deadly
accompanying images that passed,
tremulous afternoons,
dark beasts of burden,
crippled connotations,
                    blood,
nighttime conspiracies.

Here, then,
in a bad set design,
alien to thyself.

Do not listen to your step,
as it emerges above you,
above your eyes' imperfect silting,
outside the trees,
the dust presaging catastrophes,
and that hollow night that comes full of stigmata.
It's not night,
        it's not time.
It's a hospital forecourt,
a synthesis of stained shadows and cinders,
summer flies,
the drains' mire.

Better to go.
Not to see kids with granite faces in the morning,
enraged men milling in the street,
with hats low over their brows
and their furrowed necks,
rolling down to the square
and scattering into a grey horizon,

scorched skin,
           yellow eyes,
fever that comes from the trash,
flame of a silent rage,
for their souls are bound to the same trash,
the same blood,
           that which jeers at you,
fierceness, hysteria.

I reflect on this street's murderous darkening,
nine o'clock at night,
building materials, saprophytes, charred doors,
the light that appears in the window
houses hanging from the sky,
ready to fall and explode,
for years on a thread,
I want to go out, to get some air,
stillness, words, stillness, images,
those who have died
though they wanted so much to live,
all had their hands clenched
and were holding nothing,
in this street,
all died with clenched hands
or with teeth imprisoning their souls,
inhaling foul air, night and day,
in cheap sheets.

Those who have died. So many.

Unrepentantly again I cling
to a narrow circle of things,
trapped in images, such images.

(All this I lived through very young
and I can no longer be
what they call: a normal person).

                              1982

From:
FRAGMENTA
1971-1982

1
Night.
Black doves
tumble
in the sky.

2
His eyes
gagged.
A wall
in the void.

3
River
of red light.
Empty light.

4
Moon
light
of panic
planted
in fear.

5
Inside me I have
a child
with frost and clouds.

6
The sea
is raving
in its fever.

7
My fingers
pour
into space.

8
Trees, shadows, moons.
In the chasm whirs the river
and the stars' mechanism.

9
The night is here. The wind is here.
Here also and low is a cold sky.
In the wind the stars blossomed.

10
All the trees.
The iron bridge.
And the ancient cradle:
autumn.

11
Times have changed.
He has aged.
They put him in an armchair.
There he saw his blood
turning yellow.

12
To the bone.
To the tide.
Whereat the great orchestra of trees.

13
The window opened.
Like the unexpected,
like time lying in wait.

14
The wall.
The black stain on the coating.
The light turns on the streets.

15
Yard, scrap iron.
Grease and oil.
The day smelled of burnt grass.

16
Friends of old came.
The snow petrified,
the earth fell silent.
Shadows howl in the dusk.

17
Footsteps.
Old signs in the shops.
And in the river trash,
shit-stained paper.

18
Show me the way, then.
Show me your hand,
your plucked head.

19
Day is breaking,
red and grey.
Like a gelded animal
in the room.

20
Years since I was here.
Rubbing with my hand the vegetation,
smelling glass and dust.

21
He opened the fridge.
He drank some water.
He left the door open.
The night outside:
frozen cellophane.

22
Dream in the afternoon:
the blackness flashed.

23
Outside the window,
lamps in the office opposite.
The gendarme passed,
the night watchman passed.
A rag,
a void.

From:

GARDENS OF THE MOON
1983-1988

GARDEN OF THE MOON

I
I was gazing at the moon as it rose in the sky
lost in this dark plateau.
Again I recalled the sound of the glare,
the azure plain that covered my childhood.

In the whisper that shines in the opposite house
I am the one walking, and outside the autumn
like an enchanted spirit was returning to the garden.

Old the earth climbed as far as my eyes,
I saw the hills circled by fires
and to the North horses coming down
with the dusk's harness
and with mirrors in their golden eyes.
After so many years it once again smelled
of the wound of grass in the darkness.

Through the fallow opening at the back of the houses
appeared the same sky, bright blue expanse
with its birds rising, its birds plummeting.

II
When birds drink water, they see the wind
and this gazes at the plain green and blue,
image of the sky that mirrors itself,
with red ships, fish that fly,
birds that swim upon the soil
and poplars stuck in, flags of silver stone,
vanishing high in the breeze's pulse.

III
On the night I left the trains' smoke,
a damp image slid over the window
and my thought stumbled in the dark.
Blind lights besides the tracks
and dark cisterns in the orchards.
For the last time I saw the dilapidated guard post,
the black grass around the pillboxes.

A sentry with arms "present"
patrolled beneath the moon.
On my face flickered a light
like that which grows in the garden's shadows,
houses left before the window
high in the sky the shadow of the city
reflected an image that I didn't know.

The past poured like water
from the broken jug of dreams.

IV
The rock in the mountains red and blue,
feathers of birds and the whisper of leaves,
morning's diamonds on the ridges,
wolves and deer on the paths find
their way beneath the rock's constellation.
Fall a fleeting sea
with the sun's ancient emblem.

V
I was gazing at the moon as it rose in the sky,
time's disk full of grooves,
an eye that fled from the land of the blind—
this will tell the tale tonight.
The sea on one side of the wind
and on the other swept heights.

In the sea the past rises and sets.

VI
I don't know if the flash is quicker
than the wind. The garden's stone speaks
to the grass and the moon as it rises
scatters silver calyxes in the dark corners.

Playing with the light
the world shrank in our eyes.

VII
I was gazing at the moon as it rose in the sky,
nymph of fire and ice.
In the black tulip's blemishes memory
opened petals of cloud
and eternity's images blossomed.

My face a blue mask
here, without foreign eyes, without
the dark line, touching
my deepest self,
a damp model with the grass' breath,
identical to the garden with that old path,
faces pass to its other edge
extinguishing the light behind them
and the faint smile that makes time bright.

I in between and behind me the clouds,
before me trees of water and crystal,
swarms of birds that outline the breeze,
time multiplies itself,
the wind enlarges the space,
I was gazing at the moon as it brought the tide,
I gazed at the moon:
the brightest apple of the Hesperides.

1968

The evening sank in the river,
from the grass emerged half the moon,
a breeze poured into the picture frames
and a dead crater the window
gazed at the shadow, gazed at the blind man,
at the dried tobacco leaves in the warehouse.

I am a fragment of all that I encountered,
I am the star that leaps from the boat,
the music that undulates in the mind,

the dream of the river and the shadow of the mirror.

MARA'S SHADE

Deep into the night I rose from bed,
red fringes rippled in the trees
and the sky was nowhere to be seen,
only the black velvet
covering the room with its crepe.

The house journeyed in its silence
without creaking, laden with lignite,
and a breeze came in through the windows
bearing forgetting and fragments.

Ashen, you stood beside the door,
the blood on you had grown black,
what could you want in this house,
a dry leaf flung to the ends of History.

Imaginary scenes came to mind
and incidents I'd picked up from reading.
Figures from History, anthropoids,
intelligent insects embalmed in dead narrations.
"It's Mara"—I whispered without knowing
which of the two of us was alive.

Though you didn't speak.

When thought desolates the in-between
what's history—an evil myth,
algebra of the paranoid in their libraries.

Since then have come rains,
bodies have plunged into chasms,
death seals the silence,
since then have come railroads,
junkyards in space,
decisions,
agreements not kept,
banners raised
                banners lowered,
flags trampled in the mud,

steel that rises up high,
bridges of mercury in the sunset,
you turn your eyes—the perpendicular age,
a yellow equation for the great distribution,
fires and splinters,
frozen credit,
banks, galaxies, the organized world.

Still more signatures will be added
to this universe as it shrinks,
to time as it dehydrates
and you flee,
breaking the chains of blood,
setting fire to the pistons,
behind in the night,
a red dot,
decision, light, lava, labara, loot—
"Down with the house of the Labdacidae".

On the open streets
shooting
      laughing
laughing, shooting, laughing.

EURYDICE

Without the wind that sweeps
the plain, without the sleepy
setting that tilts in the darkness,
without the trees that haunt
Persephone's phantom
and that crystal which sparkles,
fire's prison,
matter's eye,
I'll erect a house
that will look on the sunset
a door to open and close to the summer,
with a marble opening
for night's sorceries
and the blind sorceress
guided by the command
that governs the stars.

I'll sway for the last time
as the country sinks.

I'll no longer hear my own voice
and the song will be
my darkest dream—
a river of hair
and of the wind's feathers.

He whom I loved will become my shadow
the dress that follows me.
His light will cover my eyes
that I might not see the moon's dragon.

Let me keep the moment when I'm
half within the passage
and the other half without
there where time turns to marble.

In this realm I'll never again exist;
my voice alone a black dove
will rise from the earth to encounter the light

before the dark seal falls,
before I hear the deep waters.

If dreams are true,
the earth and rain will leave untouched
my silver dress
that has the gleam of a knife
and the perpetuity of rock.

Here I'll keep only my name
like an old and ageless emblem;
before I become a shade among shades
with my image I'll brand the day,
with my image I'll rap the wind
and uncracked my song will exist,
will erect a great bridge of light
that he whom I loved may descend
and then conversely ascend
to the stars.

I am Eurydice,
an image of things passed,
a figure ever leaving,
a perfect mirror.

ELLIS ISLAND

The sun rose in the glass pane,
revealing part of a frayed mattress,
the green door cracked the mirror,
doves' feathers and down, pebbles.

In a corner of the mirror flashed silver threads,
the door opened, the sea appeared
against a background of murdered red
like a photo grown old in the light,
and, behind, a ship at berth,
grey smoke, passengers disembarking
with their bags, crumpled clothes,
hats, snow-capped eyes.

Time turns the crank
and through the grinding, the decayed teeth,
you hear cries, whistles, unknown tongues…
Someone looks at his watch
with the cheap aluminium strap.
Blast furnaces hid the horizon,
pre-war smoke, and in the alleys
emergency exits, uninhabited balconies,
places of rubbish and waste.

In the roasting smell and gloom
endless lines of ventriloquists
with their ungainly coats, buttoned-up shirts,
black puddles and pitted sidewalks
yet singing as their boots tread the water
a song that rends.

Life gushes through the glass pane
like wastewater from a washer.
A window sets its sights on the void,
breath yellows the wood,
blurring the glass, hiding the wind,
the bent nail sticking out—

where you'd hang your overcoat,
where for years you'd leave your hat,
as you returned and the night rushed in,
as you left and were swallowed by the day,
full of brown stains, dirty yellows,
as you wasted, Yorgos from Kalavryta,
in the kitchen's grime and hot water.

At the edge of the window a corner of the bed,
the light pierced the wall and thundered on the mirror,
the glass emptied and twinkled like an eye,
the dove entered through the door,
golden, the sea appeared behind,
and shining beneath the surface
the green door like a submerged forest.

BIOGRAPHY

Three in the morning.
A tetrapod lurks in the clock,
the message you sent never arrived,
it was a very old recording
a record played, scratched,
into its sounds came other sounds,
disrupted melodies,
ruined instruments,
figures, movements slow like dreams.

A wind blows dragging rags,
lurching in the void are
phantoms, phantasms, memories.
I'm not sure if I've ever seen
those I recall tonight.
The non-existent feeds on lies,
the past is color and illusion.
Memory is but
refusal's dress,
a way of becoming familiar
with what dies
in an alien sentiment,
that senseless cradle.

Friends come and the unity's broken,
what comes is what I recognised,
my way of recording the seasons,
of prescribing the taste of fortune.
And night, removing all limits,
the only path for escaping from the circle,
from the tyranny of the day.

Now that the waters are blooming,
now that the mud's a black nursery
where the stars' shadow grows,
where the moon's boats glide,
thought races quicker than the eye
colonizing the lands of the mind.

Fluid summer, dotted infinity,
water without water's taste,
daybreak, a red dawn
and the sun the eye of a drunk;
in the dawn's pupil the light
refined and victorious told me all.
The same light that burns the capital cities,
the resplendent mausolea.

And then the ills of civilization:
methods, aims, programs; and the papers
that are a hoax...

Amid sparks I grew up, became a man.
With a spark I exorcise fear.
Splinters of light traverse the night
fragrances of light open the space.
Fragrances, names, meteors, signals
that are contracted—here. That are subtracted.

Colors of stars,
                        cloudless skies,
glowing irons and eyes of the asphalt,
seas that glide
                        beneath my childhood years,
ships from the metropolises, lurching...

Three in the morning,
a tetrapod lurks in the clock,
lights come on and I gaze
at the grass on night's edge,
far from the land of birth—
Yet all the stars shine everywhere,
just as tonight,
three in the morning,
disrupted melodies, ruined instruments,
the message you sent never arrived
and bathing in the waters
incorruptible and pure like tears, the stars.

MANHATTAN 1984

Wide river with your shadows,
bridges that glimmer on the water,
the moon swaddled in clouds—
buildings conversing with the night.

Inverted foundations in the firmament,
high in the winds the red helicopters,
imaginary wings raise the curtain,
revealing time, emerald giant,
in the chasms, lakes and phantoms.

Traffic lights clamp the cold avenue,
in the openings above, in the sky's floor,
the blues, reds, dark purples,
in the moon's mirror
the iron laughs, the black grows white,
island that rolls down to the ocean,
discharging stone, discharging materials,
discharging yellow darkness.

Stone dissolves with the mud in the waters,
geometry theorems, ancient surveyors,
compasses, sextants, rice paper,
the night an iron emperor,
with tomorrow waving rags.

With fear and tears, with crowds and myths
the ash falling, the eyes aloft,
the eyes that construct horizons.

Constructions machine-gun the void,
the hours pass, the sea grows white,
there'll come a dawn of snow and ice,
dawn of ant, dawn of the dead,
dawn of the black planet.

OLD STORIES

Once poets dreamed
of waters, diamonds, tears-roses.
I see burnt cities in my sleep,
gutted windows, that the last rags
of the occupants might flap.

At the close of the century it's difficult to pass
from the day to dreams, the secret mountain
where electric fireflies hover.

The Devil's foot is no longer cleft
(as perhaps John Donne would have it).
Let the current halt, the mouths of sound,
the gates of fire, the outlines of death
be deadened.
Let the earth's magnetic field be reversed,
a solar wind fall upon the parliaments
and the nations' garbage unwanted,
harbors without lights on night's seabed.

Let mind's machine be lit again by the sun.

We are the children of armed peace,
televisions glare like stars in our lounges,
where do the chaffinch, woodpecker and lark belong,
let mist fall over the mountains and aerials.

Look to the universe to learn
the age of time.

In my sleep cities burn,
the cinders glow like a rabbit's fur
yet I longed for the fox's golden-red
that saw the fire and realised
that multiplication tables are nonsense and lies,
and our cities mirrors of the mind,
eerie factories, blocks of the dead,
squares buried by light
opening the great trench.

How many were lost in the trench—
unwinding the thread you won't find
the world's beginning but the end
of a dream that's grown dark.

If the earth's magnetic field is reversed
we may be able to fly
without wings and without anchors
in the sea of stars
while behind us will fade away
the marches of the dead,
lost causes,
the rat's realms,
the lights of Auschwitz.

From:
AGE
1986

FROM THE SIDE OF THE SEA

It was night when we descended the narrow path to the sea. No wind was blowing just as yesterday. Lights were mirrored in a black glass. In it we saw our faces' negatives.

Far off appeared the final flickers of a huge fire.

This is where we'll stay till morning, I said, and the others didn't speak. Another land began where the fire was fading and no one knew it. No one knew if what was burning was the great palace, as the day's rumors had it, or gleams of a glory burning in time. Someone suggested we go to find the ash remaining before the wind scattered it.

Always there's a sea intervening, said one of the others, with his voice covering his face. We, too, could start a fire and burn the sea. Glass doesn't burn and what you see is not the sea.

So it was all lies then. And who is to blame for the deceit? Leave me alone, I don't know. I don't know I tell you.

There could have been some stars. If you project the sea into the sky, you create a landscape. That glass reflects nothing, there's no light shining anywhere. Look ahead, look at the pass; the pass is one way, ahead is another.

If I said that I speak, no one would believe me. We came to be silent. The stars are the fish, and if the deep full of stars were ours. Better for me to fish in the sky, to drive away the night.

Who is the night, what is the night, left right, O left right, O would it were dawn for me to go out in the street or slip here now, who said that the sea is blue, let's whiten the sea, the sea night's cast, there is a night that is the sky, there is a night that is the deep, there is another night and infinite space as you cross the black mirror.

Honestly, I don't know. I was born with a glass eye, for you to see in there what doesn't appear. Whatever I see burns my stomach.

I think the wind is coming, yes, now I know, we came for the wind, it's our wind, no, it's the wind of others, no, it's not the wind, it's the wind's wind, it's a fragment from the palace, it's the dust from the palace's ash, it's the smoke from the queen's dress, her red perfume, no, it's the queen's groaning in the arms of her lovers. Yes, it's the wind—but it's of no matter.

If I were to jump, I'd find myself at the other edge of that sky, if I turned around. If...

If I looked at the same time now behind now in front, I'd know straightaway that the Earth was moving, yes, perhaps I'd see Galileo, if I were telescopic with his old speculum.

If I held out my arm, if I retracted my arm, if I laughed...

If I were I, if I were like you and if you weren't you but the one who's now nodding to me, if everything with one hypothesis or without hypothesis, or anyhow if we could employ some clear reasoning, if we put some limits to the game, what game, who's playing, who's marked the cards, who's Lucifer and the Angel of time, who's shedding leaves on us...

It was night when we descended the narrow path to the sea. There were no stars, no moon shining. The ruins of the fire in the palace began to set.

MARRIAGES OF THE MOON

We were at home, gazing at the moon. News came from afar, motionless shadows on the street. With the lights off, the edges of the furniture gleamed, with the clock showing an hour that had passed, with the mark opposite, fragments in the head, the eyes covered by voices.

We were down below looking high up, we were alone, only us—who remained waiting. I didn't know how many of us there were, I never counted. A roof opened to the sky, it was inhabited by the moon.

The moon, the sun of the dead...

The moon, the emblem of the loser...

The moon, a silver apple in the teeth of the night...

The moon, the woman I loved.

It inhabited the dark information: that the town had now been taken, that during the night conspirators had broken in, that those remaining would surrender from moment to moment.

We are those remaining, we are in the house. And if we can't go out, it's because the moon will betray us, our faces will show, the unknown form of each of us will shine.

It didn't rise, it sank, sat on the roof, filled the house with silver dust, the glasses gleamed, the curtains shone, the furniture moved, one of us got up, I'll climb up this ladder, he shouted, there's no other way, I can hear the footsteps, I can hear those coming, I'll take this moon with me, go to the land of the sun, I am a child of noon, I wanted to journey in vertical time, in absolute light, and not like now, a victim of reflection.

I'll become a shadow to emerge from the shadows.

I'll see the enemy through the dream-scope, we haven't seen the enemy yet, shadows are rising on the other side, the moon creates the shadows, the moon inhabits the water, above us the moon, below us the moon, this house gets up to rise to the moon, no, the moon sat on the roof, it is the same old image, it is the stamp, what I know, what I was told, what I can learn in this short life, but now the others are approaching, where are the others, the moon is the others' advance guard.

The news multiplied, the game was now lost. There's nothing left for us but this silver ball that isn't ours. What did the moon come to do tonight? To marry the night, said someone, the guests will be arriving any time, we have to leave, before the night shines, before we appear, before the light touches us.

I don't know where the white magnet is pointing, we have no direction, there's no course, everything is becoming rounded, the circle is getting smaller, the others will arrive, the others are coming, I'm not ready, I wasn't one of those who lose.

I hear the footsteps, I hear the voices, I hear the silence behind the voices, the darkness that buzzes, I hear the black insects approaching, I hear that the sun never existed, all lies, no, the sun existed, the sun exists, even if it lives elsewhere, I'll wind the clock forward, there is no clock, the clock is the moon, the time for marriage, the time for transformation, I hear the footsteps, before long the knocking, before long the opening, before long a door to tomorrow, others will burn the night, after the fire the darkness but after this fire the light, only with light will we receive light, not in the dark corners, not in the caves, not in the woods but in the plateaus, I wanted to make a shelter out of pure sky, a sea suspended over the mountains, a quiet lake of mined light, inside me remained a thunderstruck landscape, journeys come and go, that's where I belong, you know it, that's where I was always, others brought me to this land…

I put on my clothes, left my orders, closed the wardrobe, looked at my watch—I'm ready.

I bring before me my own images. Accelerating, in order to

finish before the time for sleep. I lived in the wind's nests, the sky nourished me.

Departure time, arrival time. Somewhere afar insects are crawling. I saw the birds, I saw the sky. I'll remain upright.

I continue to remain the same person.

To whom shall I give my eyes…

The moment of colors…

At great speeds…

Looking from above…

The moon descended into the room, walked over the furniture, stood at the window, then ascended to the upper floor, the boards shone, the cracks in the floor were visible. Then it began to grow, filled the entire room, the walls were almost bursting, the windows shattered, the wind rushed in thundering in the furniture and the corners, knocking was heard outside. The others smashed down the door.

From:

FRAGMENTA
1983-1988

1
Perseus's eye.
Light and diamond.
Uncut in the future
where the beast dies
gazing
at its own image.

2
Cactus flowers.
The insignificant
speaks in the light.

3
Propellers and wings,
sails made of cloud.
In the harbor
I was raised up
by the rain
of September.

4
The dirt track.
The song
sung by the light.
And the great dancer:
the river.

5
Lesson from the sun,
rustling of the leaf:
the ancient glare.

6
The light comes,
wet steel.
The tide comes.
We tumble
into the light.

7
The polar light
that you called
immortality.

8
Blue craters.
Sea.
Clouds, morning's rags.
The clarity of ice.

9
Amid the ruins
the Goddess appeared to me
one cold night.

10
A large parlor
with candlesticks.
With paintings,
with an echo.
And with an iron cloud
mounted
on the ceiling.

11
The light passes.
The glare
stained the sky.

12
In the dance's orchards
and from the dust's depths
the sea rises
a tri-color flag
blown by eternity's
glittering breeze.

13
Without the axis,
without the triangle,
without the perpendicular
and the straight line.
It's with a sail,
with a rope,
with a severed leaf
that Spring comes:
a red brushstroke
on the wall.

14
The iron creaks—
stationary years.
And the white light
that waves on the quay.

15
Like a cry,
like a clang,
like the voice that fades
the depth rises.

16
Shall I recall the sea.
Shall I imagine the smooth stone.
Let the sea open,
let the golden fish glide.

17
What am I looking for
beneath the spiders?
In what deeps
am I dreaming?

18
The light of the stars
that reveals
non-existence.

19
I was with you
even where I was
without you.

20
From afar the sound.
Ruins, foundations, years.
For all I don't know.
The dawn.
Shrouding the day.

21
Articulate cosmos
you are not mine.
You expand time,
you distort time.

22
No one comes.
No one goes.
I know the Spring:
the one flag.

23
Yesterday I saw the Goddess again.
She was even younger
after so many years.

24
Where's your black snout,
where's your eye growling,
in the wretched house,
a bone,
a rope,
a small chain.

25
George Washington Bridge
The lights go out.
Sounds of cars.
The first planes pass.
Standing on the bridge
with diamond eyes.

26
Deserted town.
Peaceful night.
Devoid of thoughts.
Scent of those absent.

27
The moon emerged,
the waters sparkled.
The machine roars,
like a person.

28
Your house is a hive,
your house is a prison
with you far from the herd
before the window,
in your ears dark wailing,
waiting for the dawn
fearful of the infinite.

29
With eyes dead
fixed on yesterday—
with a black whistle.

30
Around the architect's light
fly night's numbers-moths.
On a sheet of paper
the floor-space of the universe.

31
The fake metropolises
glitter:
cartoons
of the Labyrinth.

32
You die.
The rock lives on.

33
Night's falling,
the only news.
Time is in exile.

34
Raining
through the leaky darkness—
are remnants of the sun.
It resembles
the sound of the breeze
the damp gnawing
that rots.

35
N.Y. 1984
Here far off,
fabricated news,
worn negatives,
torn programs.

36
The blind eye:
zero.

37
I write looking for
a beginning
that I'm ignorant
of how it happened.

38
How deep are the years?
I drag up addresses—
insatiable shapes.

39
Silence.
On the window
the spider slipped.

40
You don't hear
the harbor's music.
Nor even hats, kerchiefs,
seagulls' wings.
High up here
the pulley
creaks in the dusk.
It smells of engine grease,
heavy loads,
songs
of stench.
From out of the iron
comes garbage.

41
I am a narrow passage,
a truncated ending,
a language
that confutes itself.

42
Years of the persecutor,
of the gendarme;
darkness,
tarred consciences.

43
Rags,
flags,
cries.
A light all lead dawns.
Here the small deposits,
the wretched relics.

44
The 'instantaneous' fallen.
The never remorseful,
the suddenly wretched,
the survivor.

45
The biggest act today:
to look at the horizon.

46
All things round
roll.
All things red
molt.
We're beset by grey.

47
Stars.
The moon's fish
in sleep.

48
All I care for now
is what burns
my eyes.

49
From the voice to the word,
from the word to the phrase
and from there to the utterance
that teaches you to forget.

50
We said a lot.
We said it all.
We'll devour paper.
We'll say still more.
Nothing ends.
Everything begins.
Eternally.

From:
TERRA INCOGNITA
1989-1995

DARK SUMMER

On the threshold of the West we built our towns—
blind windows, dark aquaria.

From where does the wind come
that pounds against the roofs and belfries,
against the walls and windows
damp and old like death?

The light sets
leaving its crimson rags
between the shadows
and the sky is a darkening arena.

To the North will go the victor.
To the South the ships
led by the Sun's Centaur.
And to the East
the water's agate eyes
with the springs' stars and the wind's fires.

The garden beside the river
and the sea sown with trees.
Night's silk and ebony were the roses
and the well a dark lotus
from which emerges
the shadow, the oracle and the rock,
the night that the nightingales played for us
the oratorio of the stars.

Your hair grew longer
in Berenice's hair.
From your mouth flows the sea.

Your mouth is
the wind's palace.

With the wind's warp
you wove your tunic
that I might now wipe
the ash,
the mud,
the dust,
the hubris.

On the threshold of the West we built our towns—
blind windows, dark aquaria.

Let the wind caress your face.
In the morning frost your tears
will vanish.
Beyond the deserted cemeteries,
above the sky
a great star blooms
the heart of the universe.

We'll flee with the cry and the dream
that falls like an emerald
in the darkness of the ages.
In your mythical eyes I'll again see
the sea drawing the line of the horizon,
and your breath
will enlarge the ebony leaf
that will turn to the light
just as the bee is guided
by Spring's compass.

The dream is greater than the world,
than the tyranny of speech.
For you name beauty only in whisper,
for upset, love and tears
are rare metals
not worn away by Hades' light.

Moons were the eyes of the serpent
that lived in the house of our childhood.
Its skin had the seal of old civilizations
and it was the herald's silver wand,
the ring of Beauty
and the eclipse of the Moon.

Its eyes mirrors of eternal life
above the darkness of the grave.

If the voice fades, the garden will remain.
Your lead dress will glide over the floor,
the light of your skin will shine
untouched like the Pleiad
so the objects will vanish into dust,
faces and colors will melt
and take shape again
in the depth of the inexpressible
and the golden mist from the Elysian Fields.

AFTER THE BATTLE

The battle lasted till the sun went down.
With darkness they lay down to sleep
living and dead together,
they switched on the glaring searchlights.

Tatters of darkness flapped
in the dust raised by the wind.

From the highest window
came the sound of a wedding waltz.

The dead in the ditch
lit the night.

In the main square
a steel firefly landed.
Pylades, Clytemnestra,
Aegisthus climbed out.
In the pilot's eyes I saw Orestes
gazing at the sky
then together they all vanished
in the searchlight's deadly whiteness.

We lived under the star of death.
We ate bitter bread.
In our sleep forests of lead
sprouted and thickened.

Thick dirty light.
Days of mud and bugs.

The bugs took over our homes,
made their kingdoms in the bedrooms.
They went to the graveyards,
became guards of the dead.
They built mausolea in the earth's bowels,
in the cities of Hades.

From the water's eye
the sun was born.
I'll give you my voice,
give you my eyes and skin,
speak to you with the voice of the hawk,
the flight of the sparrow,
the tap tap of the woodpecker.

The enemy entered by the north gate.
The ritual surrender took place,
flags, keys and women were handed over.

They were many.
They were known as time's usurpers.

MEDEA

Light of water and heaven's light,
you who link the upper world and lower,
who penetrate the skin
and brighten the eyes,
who make the blood glow,
the tree blossom
and the cloud smile,
give me the strength to rise from the ground.

I came here bringing with me
the distant images of older farewells
when as a child behind the crystal ball I saw
the world opening in the slow space.

Those who believed
that after the drama and disaster
I'd be left in mid-air, without homeland,
know not that I was born
of the waters and clouds
and behind my own eyes
protected and imperishable
amidst acacias and myrtles
looms eternity's fiery palace.

Mingling with men's voices
is the music of the gods;
they called it language, alphabet, myth and word.
In the words of men
my perished shape will pass
into posterity.

I came from the sea,
from the ocean's ends,
from Circe's deathly isle;
I am Medea, the black swan
who forges a path through the sunset,
a phantom over Ephesus,
the specter of sorrow behind closed windows,
nostalgia now dead.

At night with sails furled
the boat slid out to sea.
With oars raised
and masts wedged in the sky
it halted in mid-sea
forever setting its seal on time.

Yet what is time?
The wretched bane of mortals
with their campaniles and clocks,
with their sundials?

Love draws me to decay,
yet in your arms it's not my body
but the clay bugbear that leapt
from all your frightened hearts.
In your clothes you keep fear warm
and your towns are the unseen's spells,
and your dwellings logarithms of ruins.

Houses fashioned from the Dragon's tooth
that looms over the roofs.
The streets are its petrified hair
and below its eyes its generation formicates.

I needed neither thread nor paint,
my homeland is the infinite my home the spring,
the blue stream of time
where unaltered flows my face.

I always was, did not become.
A day is an entire life
since time does not exist
and one life is never one.

I am the life beneath death's cloth.
I live beyond light and conscience.

The metal of the seasons
that shines in the heavens
is me.

The leaf that turns to the light
and provokes the infinite
is me.

I am the daughter of the Sun
that shines over the dark bed
and the spark setting fire to the Nether World.

I am the seabird
that on the waves inscribes
the book of tomorrow's world.

I am the feather that slowly falls
on desire's invisible edge;
the purple sheet that slipped from the sunset
into the garden's lull;
my eyes are two beads
of fire and reverie
in which the cosmos throbs,
rose of rock and light that opens and closes,
voice, soul, dust of water and asbestos,
as the world became mine in a day,
as I wanted not to learn but to take,
as I Medea, goddess,
a solitary North Star
in the Mediterranean sun,
I who wanted but doubted,
I who desired and took
on a path of no return,
I appeared for a day,
for a year,
an aeon
and an eternity.

What's passed, has remained.
What's remained and what's vanished.

I brought into this world the heaviest light.
Men called it darkness and lament.

RETURN I

Unmoving, the light like a dream turned to stone—
far from us the wood darkened.

Here again, after years that flowed by,
slowly rowing upon the waters' iron mirror.

A sparrow stood at the window
and looked at the day,
this is not the town where you were born
with the tarnished river
now disappeared in the mountains
and the fallen star of your youth
that oxidizes the rock.

Lift the mirror.
Beneath the material
is a key that opens the door
to the garden with the bees
and the waters
shining black in Hades' fountain.

We're strangers, both here and elsewhere,
we're strangers and ill-matched
and our sole homeland a patch of ground
as the poet told you long ago
between animals and birds
in the land of the Hyperboreans.

The eyes follow the light,
two stars of solitude and silence
crowned with darkness.

What is it that dies,
who called the truth light,
who at night touched glass and fire—
and the mountains are ships
of blazing cobalt
and the islands are clouds
steered by Sagittarius.

The wind now beats on the pavements
and the buildings build an acropolis of Lethe.
Tomorrow you'll forget all you went through,
the traces will fade.
You belong to the last
of a world that's ended
the seed of ancestors who died young.

For
old age will inherit the world.

You'll go to the land where they don't speak,
with the columns of water
and the birds
thunderstruck
will shine over the waters
like the voice's diamonds
that sail on the clouds and air.

Unmoving the light like a dream turned to stone
between animals and birds,
the glow fell over the ruins—
we're strangers and ill-matched
and this return to the wet world of our youth
magic's hand-me-downs.

Tomorrow night will cover those who've gone,
the black fire will open a hole in time
and those who remained
strangers and ill-matched will pass
from deathliness of the unseen
to panspermia of the stars.

WAVES OF THE BLACK SEA

Sky is how they call night's garden
with its silver roses sinking in the waters,
you didn't know how the stars' breeze comes low
upon the waves,
the boatswain's rays and spears
and in your sleep steps from Persepolis and Pergamum.

The light breaks behind the black theater,
dark of the voice and the shimmer,
the salt's rust flashes on the Mycenaean sword
that rose in the waters and gleamed over the Propontis.

Knife of memory, I didn't see the blood in your cleaving,
death's tread, the clang and the battle.
I saw only this blade
that flashed behind the curtain
like the keel that rends the sea in two
and in the cleft of black foam my grandfather's grave,
the day that detonated,
the eye of the sea-eagle,
the tremor of the heart that becomes one
with the hum in the engine-room;
it's your heart singing the hymn of the sea,
specters of waves and waves of snow,
the light in Vatum that you didn't see,
distant Colchis
with the woman of agate coming from Aea
leaving luminous bursts behind her,

light floods the vein and the blood is azure and golden,
bird of the tempest, bird of homecoming and wailing,
born in the stars' ashes,
marble wing of Ephesus,
how the marble travels,
how the granite gleams,
weeds of the water, valleys of citron,
gazing long at the sea to discern
whether what shines on the bottom
is Jason's tear or solitaire,
the captain's engagement ring or love's diamond clasp.

The ship travels not on the sea but the sky
between the constellations of Centaurus and Canis Major,
in your eyes some other fleece,
of silver that holds time's shavings
holds the dolphins' dreams and warriors' dead laughter,
a crimson sea now shines on the horizon
and in the cloud's cavern
the hoarse breath of water is heard.

I have a star of my own where the heart is,
a tiny glass semaphore in the depth of sleep
and beside it pass dreams, steps and flashes—
now I hear you rising in the forest of coral,
in this sea I dreamed of the lakes that I saw as a child,
the eyes of Hera,
the cloud on the apple,
Spring with spear and shield at the carnage's depot,
unready I slowly return,
the curtain opens and closes,
how many names the light has,
how can you name the light you don't see,
how in your dark tunnel
Myrmidons, Argonauts, Cossacks and Praetorians
crawl slowly in their silk garments,
how the eyes soften the metals' glare,
how the light rests like eiderdown on the gaze,
on an image that noiselessly passes before you
and lights the other depths
with the light of the rain and rock.

It's a ladder on the waters
that rises and touches Orion.
It sinks in the Propontis,
comes, goes and gets ever nearer
like persistent dreams.
It's the ladder of secrets
by which the moon descends
and secretly enters Endymion's dreams.
Time brings it nearer
now that I've learned
that heart, light and homeland are one.

I

The metal's sheen, that cold and obvious truth. The colors of the mind together with the instruments on the third tier of the orchestra. And the blind division of the seasons.

II

The cosmic gloom has become his inner life.

III

Every New Year I dream of Jacob's Ladder.

IV

I love the rain. It renders the world invisible. It renders the invisible world visible.

V

In the damp night. That's where feelings are. There with open eyes, there with closed too. Dreamlike everything depicts your mind, as in those Renaissance studios that you imagine coming to life in the tranquility.

VI

Winter's shiny clouds. Sky: image of a mundane glory. I put some music on the stereo so there'd be light in the loudspeakers. The depth that etches without thought, with the sea wherein is everything the water holds sacred. Thetis, the golden apple, the mind's dolphins. Mind where are you burning, invisible homeland. Heart of the deep. We are wet and don't know it. A firm sea with seaweed in the blood.

VII

A shadow on the brow, dust from the stars, silver of the ether, silver of the East that couples the rose and the lotus—everything passes. Everything. Under full sail in the blood with its inner breeze. Everything comes. I switched on to listen to Shostakovich's Fifteenth. Music of one Speechless where the mourning severs his arm. The strings bring your innards to your mouth.

VIII
Dull, leaden day. I was listening to Venetian music. Salutatory, polyphonic, deadly.

IX
Calm, everywhere calm: the power of inertia.

X
Nightmarish imagination: you are not yourself, you are not, you are not.